RODD RACER

TOBY CYPRESS

A PUNK ROCK * JAZZ PRODUCTION

copyright 2010

For My Friends, and Family

Written, Illustrated by
TOBY CYPRESS

PUNKROCK*JAZZ PRODUCTIONS

rodd racer, and artwork copyright 2010 toby cypress, and punkrock*jazz productions.
no material may be reproduced without written permission by t.cypress, and publisher.

RODD RACER
ISBN: 978-1-60706-387-2
First Printing

June 2011. Published by Image Comics, Inc. Office of publication: 2134 Allston Way, 2nd Floor, Berkeley, CA 94704. Copyright © 2011 Toby Cypress. All rights reserved. Rodd Racer™ (including all prominent characters featured herein), its logo and all character likenesses are trademarks of Toby Cypress, unless otherwise noted. Image Comics® and its logos are registered trademarks of Image Comics, Inc. No part of this publication may be reproduced or transmitted, in any form or by any means (except for short excerpts for review purposes) without the express written permission of Image Comics, Inc. All names, characters, events and locales in this publication are entirely fictional. Any resemblance to actual persons (living or dead), events or places, without satiric intent, is coincidental.

Printed in the U.S.A.

For information regarding the CPSIA on this printed material call: 203-595-3636 and provide reference # EAST – 379377

IMAGE COMICS, INC.
Robert Kirkman - chief operating officer
Erik Larsen - chief financial officer
Todd McFarlane - president
Marc Silvestri - chief executive officer
Jim Valentino - vice-president
Eric Stephenson - publisher
Todd Martinez - sales & licensing coordinator
Sarah deLaine - pr & marketing coordinator
Branwyn Bigglestone - accounts manager
Emily Miller - administrative assistant
Jamie Parreno - marketing assistant
Kevin Yuen - digital rights coordinator
Tyler Shainline - production manager
Drew Gill - art director
Jonathan Chan - senior production artist
Monica Garcia - production artist
Vincent Kukua - production artist
Jana Cook - production artist
www.imagecomics.com

International Rights Representative: Christine Meyer (christine@gfloystudio.com)

ALEXANDER 'THE GREAT' D E C E A S E D 	FLIPPED HIS CAR SEVEN TIMES BEFORE LANDING IN A CROWD OF 20,000 SPECTATORS. HE'S ALWAYS SAID THAT'S HOW HE WOULD LEAVE RACING. 12 CASUALTIES THAT DAY. 
'BARON' RAYMOND VON BRAUN D E C E A S E D 	DIED WHEN HE SLAMMED INTO A PILEUP OF RACERS...BECAUSE HE REFUSED TO INSTALL BRAKES. HE ONCE SAID "BRAKES WOULD JUST TEMPT ME TO USE THEM". TURNS OUT HIS BRAKES SIMPLY FAILED. 
'SCORCHY' MCNEILL D E C E A S E D 	VEERED OFF A STORMY BRIDGE, INTO THE ICY RIVER BELOW TO AVOID A FANATIC THAT JUMPED IN FRONT OF HER WITH A MARRIAGE PROPOSAL IN A PROMOTIONAL STUNT. SHE WAS LATER MARRIED TO HER PROMOTER...POSTHUMOUSLY. 
'BOMBER' BLAKEY D E C E A S E D 	DIED IN A NITRO EXPLOSION DURING AN EXHIBITION CELEBRATING HIS RETIREMENT FROM RACING. OFFICIALS BLAME "FAULTY TUNING". THE TRUTH IS STILL A MYSTERY, BUT MOST BLAME SABOTAGE. BLAKEY DIED AS THE GREATEST RACER OF ALL TIME. 

"We applaud the sweet science of a brutal craft.
Thunder Alley, where a man knows no fear for he is a gladiator whose engine his heart, his car his sword, and the streets his arena.
A craft practiced by those with nothing to lose.
Today I applaud, for I am witnessing a brutal craft...and because I have no other choice."
 -Mickey 'Mack' Beltower (writer)
  City Report 1936 Thunder Alley Rally

'GENESIS'
-JUSTICE

RODD RACER

THUNDER ALLEY. THE CITY'S BIGGEST EVENT IN RACING. OVERHEAD GAS FILLED ZEPPELINS BROADCAST THE DERBY ACROSS THE CITY.

3 LAPS THROUGH THE CITY'S WINDING STREETS, AND TUNNELS.

NO RULES,

WE STRAP OURSELVES INTO HOT RODS POWERED BY NITROUS OXIDE FUEL. STUFF SO DANGEROUS...MANY RACERS CATCH FIRE AT THE STARTING LINE.

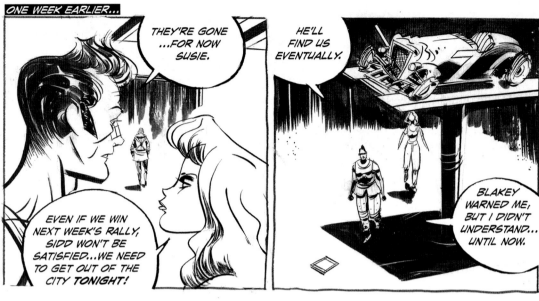

A FEW YEARS AGO, SUSIE AND I NEEDED HELP TO SAVE THE GARAGE AND CONTINUE RACING. SIDD SPONSORED OUR TEAM WHEN NOBODY ELSE WOULD.

BUT I'VE BEEN ON A BAD LOSING STREAK AND NOW I'M WORTH MORE TO SIDD SMEARED ACROSS THE TRACK.

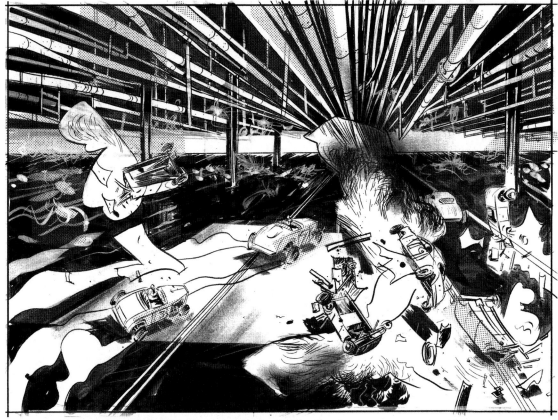

BEFORE SHE WAS **DRAG'ON**, SHE WAS **KAZI HIROTOMO** ...ONE OF THE BEST YOUNG RACERS IN DERBY. RACING WAS THE ONLY THING THAT EVER MATTERED TO KAZI, AND SHE WAS WILLING TO RISK **ANYTHING** TO WIN.

WHILE CLOSING ON A RECORD BREAKING **THIRTEENTH** STRAIGHT VICTORY, KAZI GOT SLOPPY. HER NITRO TANK BLEW...SENDING HER INTO A TURN AT **300 MPH**.

KAZI BARELY SURVIVED THE CRASH. CRIPPLED. FLATTENED. TORN. SHE MIGHT **NEVER** RACE AGAIN.

DETERMINED, KAZI TURNED TO THE **YAKUZA GANGSTERS** FOR HELP...AND THE YAKUZA TURNED KAZI INTO- **DRAG'ON**

IN EXCHANGE FOR FUNDING HER **BIONIC TWITCH REFLEXES** ...ALLOWING KAZI TO RACE AGAIN... **DRAG'ON** IS RACING'S DEADLIEST RACER AS THE YAKUZA'S HIRED HITMAN.

FUELED ON **REVENGE**, HIRED TO **KILL**...DRAG'ON IS A **GHOST** HAUNTING THE TRACKS IN PURSUIT OF **GLORY**.

GAH... TEAR GAS!!
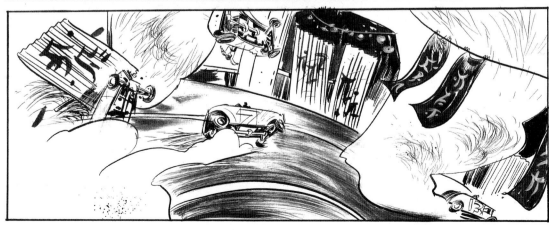

PRESENT

CAN'T SEE! THE TEAR GAS IS STICKING TO EVERYTHING!!

GOTTA LOSE THE HEADGEAR!! GET SOME AIR!

I THINK I SEE SOME ROOM UP AHEAD!

'THE FREEDOM RIDER'
-ART BLAKEY, AND THE JAZZ MESSENGERS

SUSIE WAS RAISED ON A RACE TRACK.

WHEN SHE WAS A CHILD, HER FAMILY OPERATED ONE OF RACING'S MOST FAMOUS RACING COMPANIES DESIGNING WINNING ENGINES.

ONE WEEKEND, HER FATHER BOARDED A CARGO PLANE WITH HIS LATEST TOP SECRET ENGINE DESIGN FOR A MEETING WITH INVESTORS...

BUT SUSIE LOST HER FAMILY WHEN THE PLANE CRASHED INTO THE SIDE OF A MOUNTAIN ON A REMOTE PACIFIC ISLAND. THE REMAINING INVESTORS TOOK OVER PRIMARY OPERATIONS OF THE RACING TECHNOLOGY. SUSIE LOST EVERYTHING.

SHE GREW UP TO BE A TOP MECHANIC MENTORED BY BLAKEY...

I MET SUSIE WHEN THEY TOOK ME INTO THEIR TEAM AS THEIR NEW RACER. A FEW YEARS LATER, SHE WOULD HAVE TO WATCH BLAKEY DIE ON THE TRACK.

LAST NIGHT, SUSIE REBUILT THE ENGINE HER FATHER SPENT HIS **ENTIRE LIFE** DESIGNING.

LET'S GO WIN A RACE.

'SABOTAGE'
-BEASTIE BOYS

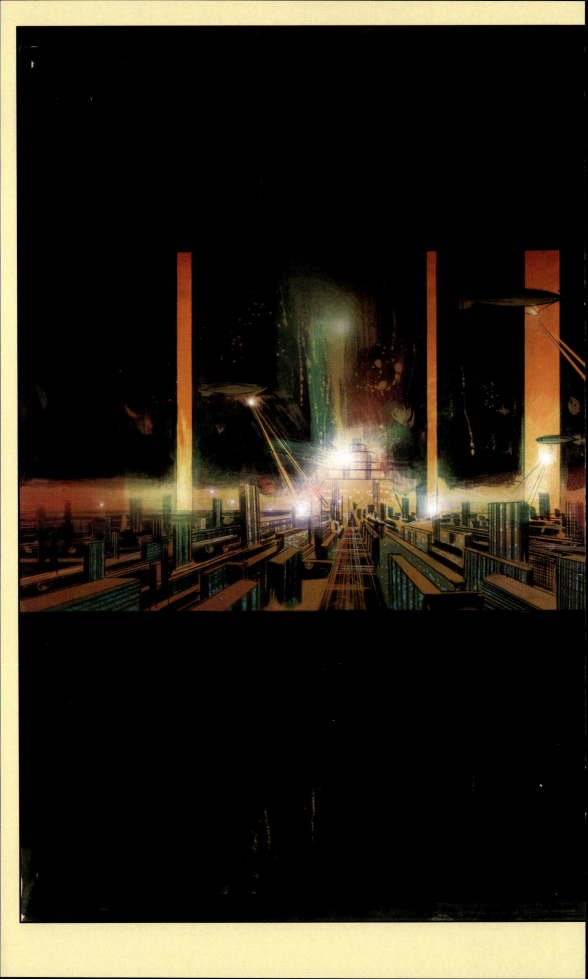

'THIS DUST MAKES THAT MUD'
-LIARS

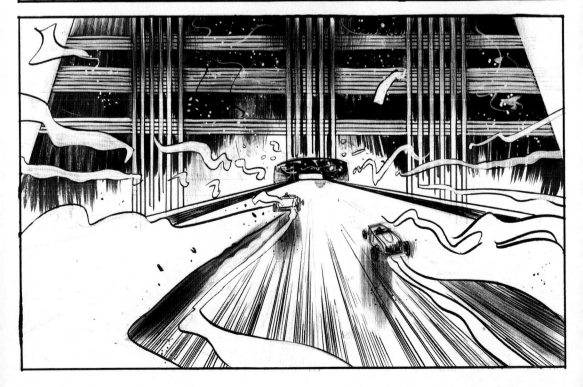

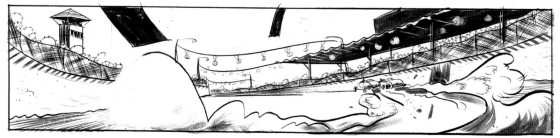

'SOLEA'
-MILES DAVIS

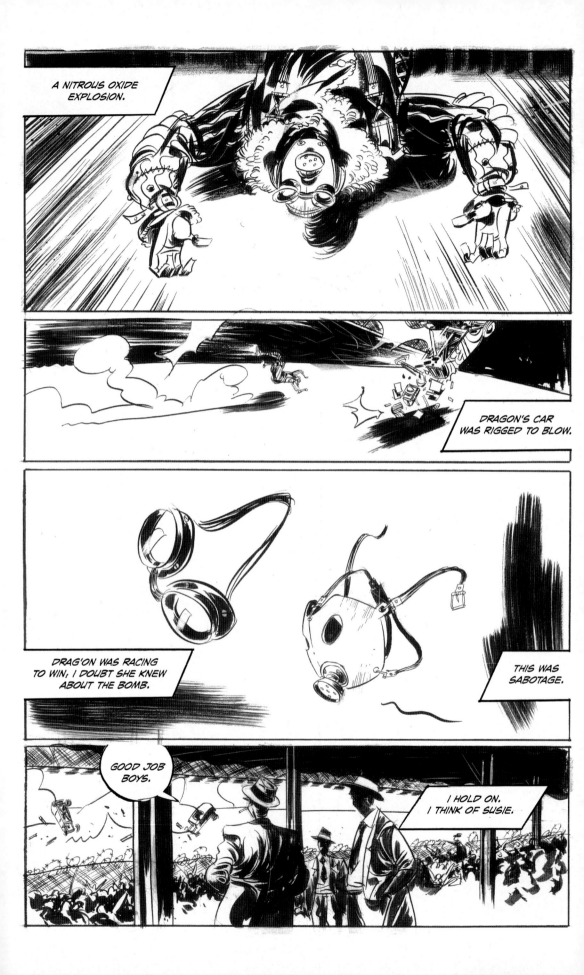

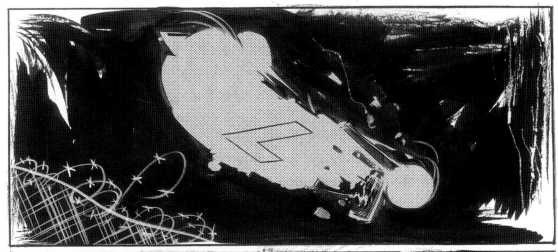

HOLD ON

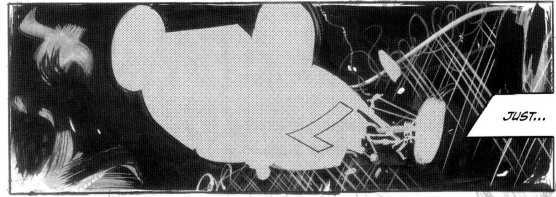

JUST...

...DON'T LET GO.

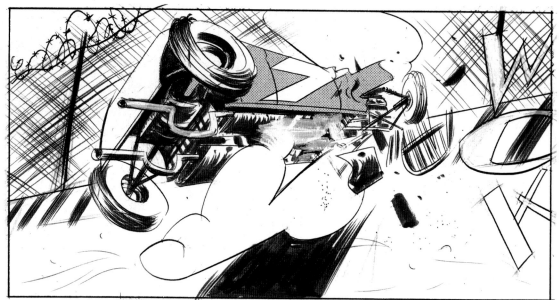

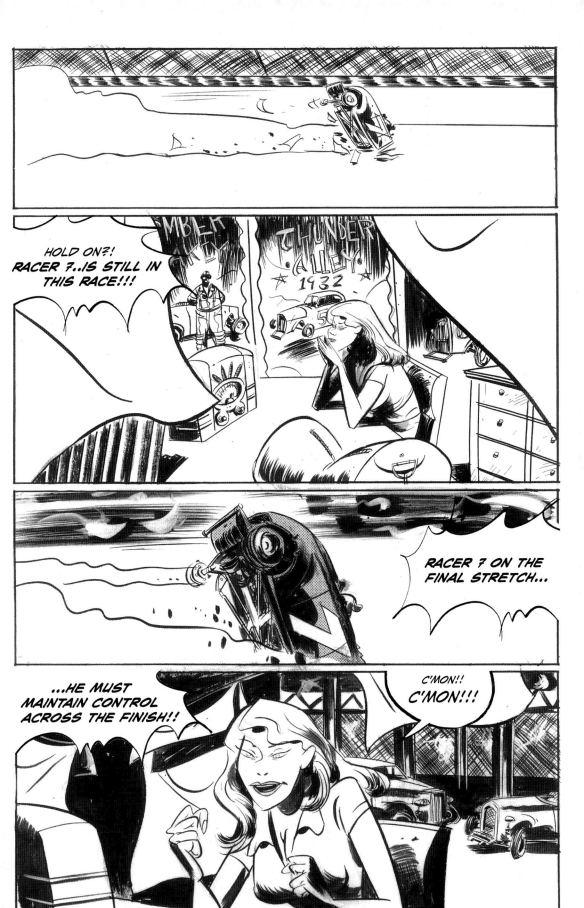

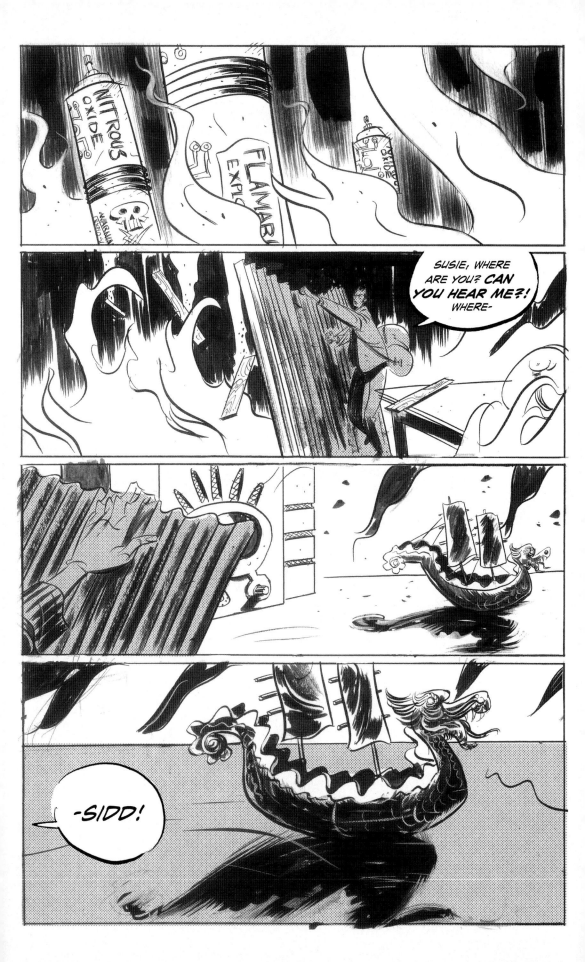

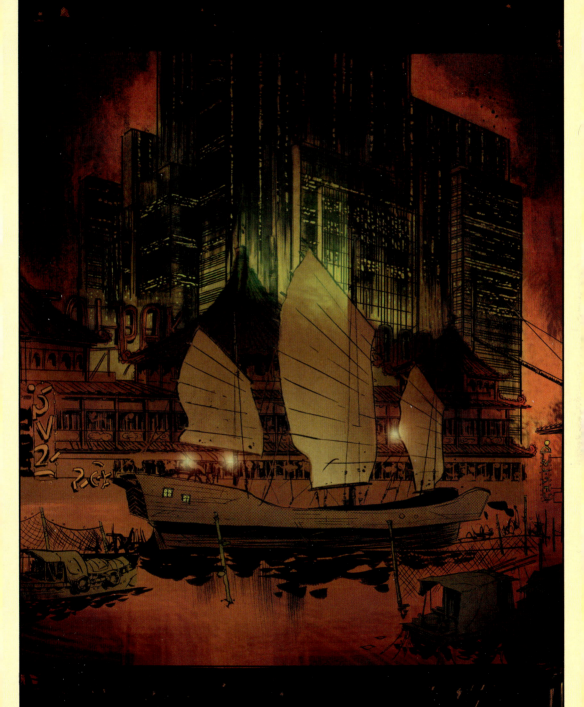

ALEXANDER 'THE GREAT'
DECEASED

FLIPPED HIS CAR SEVEN TIMES BEFORE LANDING IN A CROWD OF 20,000 SPECTATORS. HE'S ALWAYS SAID THAT'S HOW HE WOULD LEAVE RACING. 12 CASUALTIES THAT DAY.

'BARON' RAYMOND VON BRAUN
DECEASED

DIED WHEN HE SLAMMED INTO A PILEUP OF RACERS...BECAUSE HE REFUSED TO INSTALL BRAKES. HE ONCE SAID "BRAKES WOULD JUST TEMPT ME TO USE THEM". TURNS OUT HIS BRAKES SIMPLY FAILED.

'SCORCHY' McNEILL
DECEASED

VEERED OFF A STORMY BRIDGE, INTO THE ICY RIVER BELOW TO AVOID A FANATIC THAT JUMPED IN FRONT OF HER WITH A MARRIAGE PROPOSAL IN A PROMOTIONAL STUNT. SHE WAS LATER MARRIED TO HER PROMOTER...POSTHUMOUSLY.

'BOMBER' BLAKEY
DECEASED

BLAKEY DIED BECAUSE GREATNESS COMES WITH ITS ENEMIES.

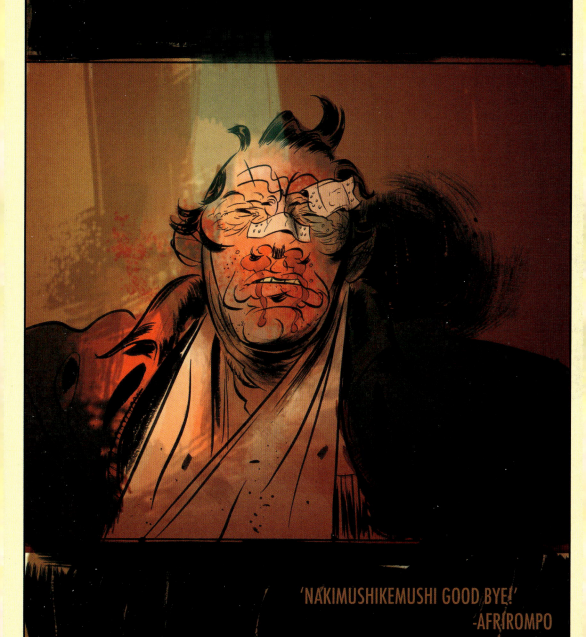

'NAKIMUSHIKEMUSHI GOOD BYE!'
-AFRIROMPO

10.

'HELP I'M ALIVE'
-METRIC

11.

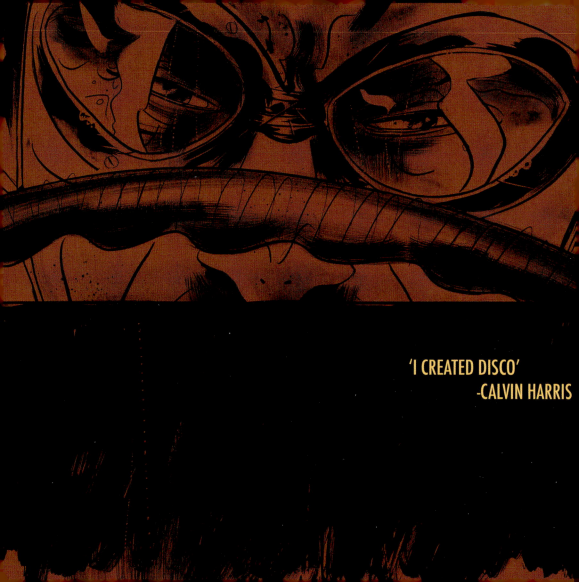

ACKNOWLEDGMENTS

'POP POP' BREWER- THANK YOU FOR YOUR GUIDANCE
MOM- THANK YOU FOR ENCOURAGING ME.
MY LOVELY SISTERS, KNOEL, AND JIMBO.
DAVID 'BONES' DELLORUSSO- A GREAT FRIEND, THANK YOU.
ALEXT TOTH, JORGE ZAFFINO, ORSON WELLES, FRITZ LANG,
PHIL AMARA, MARK CHIARELLO, ART BLAKEY, THE MISFITS, HUGO PRATT,
NOEL SICKLES, ARCHIE GOODWIN, JOE KUBERT, JOEL NAPRSTEK.
A SPECIAL THANKS TO DEBBIE, SARAH, AND LENORE AT STORE #268

A VERY SPECIAL THANK YOU
TO ALL THE AMAZING FOLKS WHO PURCHASED
RODD RACER NYCC EDITION, SDCC EDITION, AND HOLIDAY 2010 EDITIONS
YOU HAVE SUPPORTED THIS BOOK, AND MADE IT ALL POSSIBLE.

THANK YOU
TO THOSE OF YOU WHO HAVE PURCHASED THE IMAGE COMICS RE-RELEASE
OF RODD RACER.

A VERY, VERY SPECIAL THANK YOU
TO IMAGE COMICS.

TOBY CYPRESS
PUNKROCKJAZZ@GMAIL.COM

BLOGS:
WWW.TOBYCYPRESS.BLOGSPOT.COM
WWW.RODDRACER.BLOGSPOT.COM
WWW.KURSKCOMICS.BLOGSPOT.COM

ORIGINAL ART FOR SALE:
WWW.GOTSUPERPOWERS.COM
OR EMAIL- PUNKROCKJAZZ@GMAIL.COM

BOOKS
THE TOURIST-image comics
KILLING GIRL-image comics
SWALLOW BOOK4-idw publishing

SKETCHBOOK SECTION

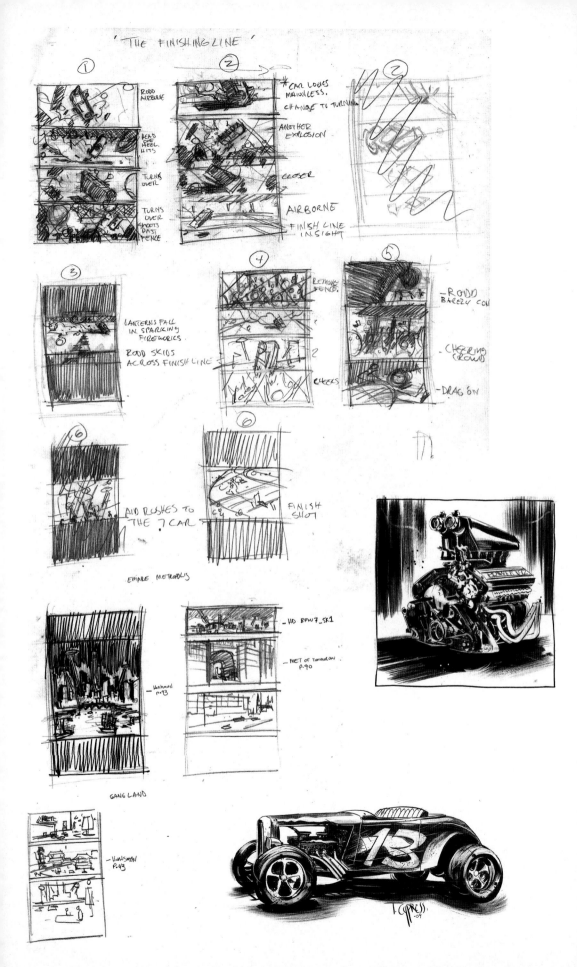